Gail and Ben can not
get home.
The lake is wide.

"We can make a
boat," said Ben.
"We can use the pail,"
said Gail.

“The pail is too big,”
said Ben.
“A nut will make
a fine boat.”

"We can nail the sail
to the pole," said Gail.

Gail and Ben set sail
in the boat.

It was wet in the boat.

"See the hole,"
said Gail.
"The boat has a hole
in it."

"Take the cap,"
said Ben.
"We can use it
to bail."

Gail did bail, but
the hole was too big.

“I see rain,” said Gail.

The rain came.
"The sail is in the lake,"
said Gail.
"We can not go."

Tim was in the lake.
"Wait," said Gail.
"Tim can save us."

Tim came up
to the boat.
"I will save you,"
he said.

“Take his tail,”
said Gail.
“Get on top,”
said Tim.

Gail and Ben rode
on top of Tim.

“Tim got us home,”
said Gail.
“Tim is a fine boat,”
said Ben.